PEGASUS ENCYCLOPEDIA
MARINE REPTILES

CONTENTS

What are reptiles?... 3

Evolution of reptiles 5

What are marine reptiles?... 7

Classification 8

Habitat 11

Food 13

Characteristics 14

Some well-known marine reptiles 18

Some extinct marine reptiles 26

Test Your Memory... 31

Index... 32

Evolution of reptiles

Around 230 million years ago, during the Triassic Period, new, larger reptiles—the first dinosaurs evolved, and dominated earth for 160 million years, until they were wiped out during the Cretaceous-Tertiary extinction event 65 million years ago.

Both mammals and birds have evolved out of reptiles. All three are part of a group called Amniota, which have been the dominant land vertebrates for over 340 million years, since the Carboniferous era.

The first reptiles originated about 320–310 million years ago during the Late Carboniferous Period. The oldest known reptile called Hylonomus lived 315 million years ago. Hylonomus was a small, 8-12 in long lizard like creature that probably fed on insects.

During the Mesozoic era, also known as the **Age of Reptiles,** a mass extinction cleared the way for the reptiles to become dominant.

Another later mass extinction event would in turn make it possible for the Age of Mammals to follow; the age we live in today. It should however be stressed that there are still considerably more reptile species on the planet than mammal species.

MARINE REPTILES

with a second hole located higher on the skull. Diapsids and later anapsids are classed as the 'true reptiles'. Turtles have been traditionally believed to be surviving anapsids due to their skull structure.

Early in the period, the diapsids reptiles split into two main lineages, the **archosaurs** (ancestors of crocodiles and dinosaurs) and the **lepidosaurs** (predecessors of modern snakes, lizards, and tuataras). Both groups remained lizard-like and relatively small and inconspicuous during the Permian Age.

Anapsids, Synapsids and Diapsids

The first reptiles were **Anapsids**, having a solid skull with holes for only nose, eyes, spinal cord etc. Soon after the first reptiles appeared, they split into two branches. One branch, **Synapsids** (including both mammal-like reptiles like crocodiles, and modern, extant mammals), had one opening in the skull roof behind each eye. The other branch, **Diapsids**, possessed a hole in their skulls behind each eye, along

The largest sea turtle ever found was close to 1,500 pounds and 28 in long. The muscles in their bodies are stronger than those of humans. Some sea turtles can travel up to 2092 km in a single day when migrating. This is based upon tracking devices researchers have placed on some of them.

What are marine reptiles?

Marine reptiles are reptiles which have adapted themselves to live in aquatic waters. The earliest marine reptiles were found in the Permian period during the Palaeozoic era. During the Mesozoic era, many reptile groups had adapted themselves for life in the seas. Some familiar groups which had adapted themselves were ichthyosaurs, plesiosaurs, placodonts and mosasaurs. After the first mass extinction at the end of the Cretaceous Period, marine reptiles had become less numerous. They consisting largely of sea turtles, sea snakes, marine iguanas and some species of crocodilians. Some marine reptiles, such as ichthyosaurs and mosasaurs, rarely stepped on the land. However, they gave birth in water. But sea turtles and saltwater crocodiles returned to the shore to lay their eggs.

> **Plesiosaurs were carnivorous marine reptiles with flippers resembling those of the sea turtles and had extremely long necks, bearing small heads. They appeared during the Jurassic Period. (200-150 million years ago) and went extinct at the same time with the dinosaurs.**

MARINE REPTILES

Classification

Reptiles are among the most diverse animals on the planet; they can be found in deserts, jungles and in water. Marine reptiles constitute a large part of the reptile family and have gone through several evolutionary adaptations that allow them to survive in water, from webbed feet to streamlined bodies. Though there are dozens of specific marine species, they can be found in four larger groups.

Living marine reptiles are distributed throughout tropical and subtropical oceans and include about 70 species

of sea snakes, 7 sea turtle species, the Saltwater Crocodile and the Galapagos Marine Iguana. Each of these groups have unique characteristics and adaptations for life in the ocean, but all must return to the surface to breathe air. Most marine reptiles must spend at least part of their life cycle in terrestrial environments to reproduce.

Sea Snakes

These reptiles spend most or all of their time at sea. Some are so well adapted to life in the water that they have lost the ability to move effectively on land. They are all air breathing, so they need to come to the surface to breathe. They feed mainly on fish and all are venomous, some deadly.

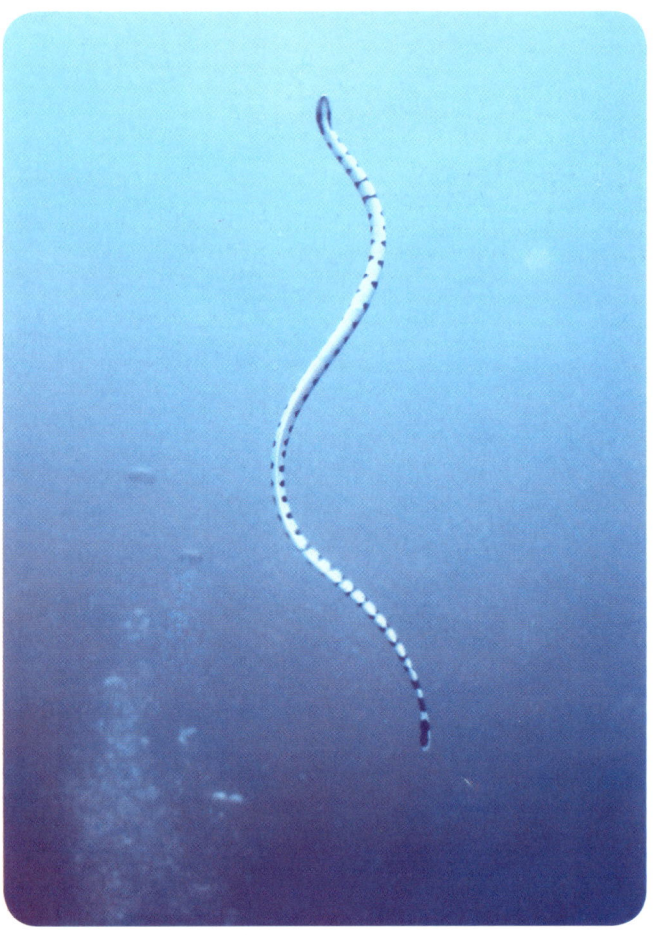

Turtles are the only group of reptiles that do not have teeth. Instead, they have a strong horny beak that is good at crushing hard food.

Classification

Sea turtles can stay underwater without surfacing to breathe for up to two hours while resting. They must surface frequently when active.

Marine Iguana

Galapagos Marine Iguanas are the only living lizard species known to forage almost entirely in the sea. Endemic to the Galapagos Islands, Marine Iguanas have spread throughout the entire archipelago, where they spend the majority of their time basking on the rocky coastline and foraging in the sea and tidal areas for seaweed and algae. Marine Iguanas are capable of staying submerged up to 30 minutes at depths of 10 m, but such prolonged dives makes them vulnerable to predators such as sharks and large fish. Consequently, they also tend to feed on exposed rocks in tidal areas, which are warmer than the deeper seawater.

Saltwater Crocodile

The Saltwater Crocodile is the largest of all living reptiles. It can be over 4.1 to 5.5 m long, and weigh as much as 800 kg! Enormous adults will eat anything they can grab, including humans and fully grown water buffalo! They are found from Northern Australia to India, and spend some of their time in estuaries and some time far out at sea. There are only one or two human deaths per year in Australia, but hundreds are thought to be killed by these crocodiles every year in the rest of their range. The only natural enemies of an adult Saltwater Crocodile are Tiger and Great White Sharks and other adult crocodiles!

MARINE REPTILES

Sea Turtles

There are seven species of sea turtles alive today, and they are found in all the world's oceans except the Arctic Ocean. The seven species of living sea turtles that are currently recognized by science are the Green Turtle, the Hawksbill Turtle, Kemp's Ridley Turtle, Loggerhead Turtle, Olive Ridley Turtle, Flatback Turtle and the Leatherback Turtle. Sea Turtles range in size from less than 100 pounds (Kemp's and Olive Ridley Sea Turtles) to between 1,300 and 2,000 + pounds (Leatherbacks). All sea turtles have streamlined bodies and large flippers, enabling them to swim gracefully, covering hundreds or even thousands of miles during migrations between nesting beaches and marine feeding areas.

The Green Turtle can be found in all tropical and sub-tropical waters, both in the Atlantic and the Pacific. All species need to come ashore to lay their eggs, and this is where they are most vulnerable. All are threatened to some extent, but the Leatherback, Kemp's Ridley and Hawksbill Turtles are listed as critically endangered.

Aquatic turtles spend most of their time in the water and then bask in the sunlight to warm up. Some spend most of their

> **Sea turtles that eat jellyfish often confuse plastic bags with jellyfish. This is very harmful to their digestive system. It is therefore very important to these creatures and many others that we do not litter.**

time in lakes or swamps while others, like sea turtles or leatherback turtles, traverse the oceans and typically only venture onto land to lay their eggs. Turtles are distinguished by their shells, which offer them protection from predators. Some, like painted turtles, have webbed feet that allow them to both swim through the water and dig, while others, like sea turtles, have flippers that help propel them through the ocean.

Habitat

If asked to imagine a reptile, most people will think of lizards sunning in the desert, snakes slithering through the jungle, or geckos skittering in the corners of a human home. However, many reptiles spend their days gliding through tropical waters and migrating throughout the world's oceans.

Home of Sea Turtles

Some sea turtle species range in warm oceans worldwide, while others are limited to certain oceans or regions. Greens, Leatherbacks and Loggerheads can be found in all oceans, except at the poles. Hawksbill Turtles also range worldwide, but are found primarily in the tropical reef habitats in the Caribbean and in tropical Australia. The Flatback is also found in Australian waters. Kemp's Ridley is an Atlantic turtle, preferring the western North Atlantic, while the Olive Ridley calls the Pacific Ocean its home.

Marine Iguanas of the Galapagos

The Marine Iguana is native to the Galapagos Islands off the coast of Ecuador. These scary looking herbivores can grow up to 1.7 m long and use their sharp teeth to scrape algae off of rocks. Unfortunately, human-introduced predators such as rats and dogs are threatening these fascinating creatures. The Marine Iguana is considered vulnerable to extinction.

Astonishing fact

Green Turtles can migrate more than 1,400 miles to lay their eggs!

MARINE REPTILES

A sea turtle cannot retract its limbs, head or neck under its shell like a land turtle. The shell adaptations necessary for retractile limbs would impede rapid swimming.

Home of the Sea Snakes

Sea snakes can be found throughout the tropical waters of the world from Africa to Southeast Asia to Panama. There are over 65 species in the ocean and all are highly poisonous. Sea snakes have one of the most toxic venoms known in all snake's species. As active predators, the sea snake diet consists mostly of small fish found on coral reefs. Many species spend their entire lives at sea, although they tend to be found in shallow waters.

Home of Saltwater Crocodiles

Saltwater Crocodiles are found in Southeast Asia and Northern Australia. During the wet season, they spend their time in freshwater swamps and rivers but during the dry season, they move down stream to estuaries and can sometimes be seen in the open sea.

Some say that the Saltwater Crocodile is an animal most likely to eat a human. This marine reptile can reach up to 6 m and weigh up to 1,300 kg. It is the largest crocodilian in the world. Although they can swim far out to sea to feast on sharks, their prey mostly includes land-dwelling monkeys, boars and wild buffalo. They are considered at a low risk for extinction. However, hunting and habitat loss has put pressure on their populations.

Food

The Galapagos Marine Iguana feeds almost entirely on algae (seaweed) that is found between the tide-lines or below the sea's surface. Its food consists of small red or green algae.

Sea Turtles eating habits may change as they age. For example, from the time Green Turtles hatch, to the time they attain juvenile size, they are mainly carnivorous. After this stage, they progressively shift to a herbivorous diet. Green Turtles, and probably Flatbacks, are primarily vegetarian. Loggerheads like jellyfish, shrimp, clam, and mollusc, while Leatherbacks like soft-bodied animals like jellyfish.

Most sea snake species have toxic venom for quickly immobilizing the fish, eels and crustaceans that make up their diet. In a few species that are specialised fish egg eaters, the venom and the fangs are degenerated and non-functional. Other species have become highly specialised in their diet and only eat a single type of prey, such as eels, gobies or catfish. The most common species encountered in non-tropical areas, the Yellow-bellied Sea Snake, travels along on the surface with floating debris in mid-ocean and eats the small fish that associate with these rafts.

The diet of a Saltwater Crocodile is made up of a variety of prey. Adult crocodiles eat turtles, snakes, birds, crabs, wild boar, buffalo and even monkeys. The Saltwater Crocodile is an opportunistic predator, meaning it will adapt its diet to whatever prey is available in its environment that meets its dietary requirements.

Astonishing fact

Green Sea Turtles can stay under water for as long as five hours. Their heart rate slows to conserve oxygen; nine minutes may elapse between heartbeats.

Characteristics

All reptiles share some characteristics. Though most of these features are present in most of the reptiles, some features might be present in some and absent in some.

Dry skin with scales

Reptiles have dry skin with scales or scutes. Scutes are large bony plates present on the animal's skin as in a tortoise or an armadillo. Reptile scales may be small and overlapping, as in many lizards, or large and adjoining, as in turtles. The skin of a reptile has few glands and high levels of keratin (a sort of protein), which prevents water loss through the skin. The scales and scutes are formed from the epidermis and are made of keratin, to protect the body.

Well developed body systems

All reptiles have vertebrate with a strong skeletal system and a rib cage. They have a well-developed brain and a central nervous system. A pelvic region with a minimum of two spinal bones is also present in most reptiles.

> In lizards and snakes, the scales do not increase in size as the animal grows, the old scales must be periodically shed and replaced by a new set of larger scales. In the shedding process, also called ecdysis, the older upper layer of the skin with its attached scales loosens and breaks away from a newer layer that has developed beneath it!

Characteristics

Reptiles have lungs

Reptiles do not possess gills at any stage in their life. These animals breathe with well-developed lungs right from birth. Most of them have two lungs, except some snakes, which possess only a single lung.

Reptiles are tetrapods

Reptiles are considered as tetrapods with two sets of paired limbs. Most of these animals have five clawed toes on each limb, which are angled downward to aid faster movement. In some reptiles, like snakes, worm lizards, etc., the legs are absent, but these animals are considered to have evolved from a four-limbed ancestor.

Amniotic eggs

Reptiles are the first animals with **amniotic eggs**. These eggs can survive without water as they have protective shells and membranes that allow oxygen and other gases to pass through. Most reptiles lay eggs, but some of them give birth to young ones by hatching the eggs inside the body of the mother.

MARINE REPTILES

The Leatherback sea turtle migrates the farthest, travelling 5,000 km from its nesting place to a feeding site.

cloaca and only the remaining waste is excreted.

Offspring similar to adults

The offspring of reptiles resemble the adults at the time of birth itself. There is no transformation, as in the case of amphibians.

A three chambered heart

All reptiles have a three-chambered heart. Crocodiles are an exception however, for they have four-chambered hearts like mammals and birds.

Cloaca

The gut, the ducts of urinary and sexual organs of the reptiles lead to one posterior chamber, called the 'cloaca', which has a muscular opening at the base of the tail. In case of reptiles living in dry regions, water is further absorbed into the body from the waste in the

Characteristics

Cold blooded

Reptiles are cold-blooded. That is, they lack the ability to regulate their metabolic heat (heat derived from the oxidation, or 'burning,' of food and from other processes) for the production of sustained body warmth and a constant body temperature. Therefore, they have to maintain their body temperature by basking in the sun.

Being cold-blooded, the metabolism of reptiles is dependent on the temperature of their environment and they require less food than other animals. Some reptiles can go weeks without a meal.

Other physical features

Reptiles have keen sense organs, which help them to find food and escape from predators. Eyes are one of the most important sense organs for the reptiles. In most reptiles, these organs are located at the front of the head to facilitate binocular vision. While most of the different types of lizards can move each eye independently, some of them have a protective cover above the eyes.

Some well-known marine reptiles

Flatback Sea Turtle

The Flatback Sea Turtle is named so for its flattened carapace (shell). The flatback's olive gray shell is elliptical in shape with upturned edges. The ventral side, or plastron, is pale yellow. The shell measures between 102-125 cm and these turtles weigh about 84 kg. The flatback's smooth, waxy shell is quite thin and easily damaged.

Flatbacks are unique in many ways including their choice of habitat. Instead of clear, coastal waters, flatbacks live in turbid, inshore waters.

The flatback turtle is indigenous to Australian waters and is not found anywhere else in the world. They inhabit the coastal waters of Western, Northern and Eastern Australia.

Like many sea turtles, the flatback has a varied diet that includes squid, sea cucumbers, soft corals and mollusks.

Flatback sea turtles are preyed upon by saltwater crocodiles, dingoes, foxes, rats, and monitor lizards attack their hatchlings. Inshore, herons and sea eagles are known to prey upon them as well.

Some well-known marine reptiles

Kemp's Ridley Sea Turtle

Kemp's Ridley Sea Turtles are the most critically endangered of all sea turtles and are currently on the Endangered Species list. These gentle reptiles are known to nest only along the coast of Mexico and recently, Texas. Besides having a limited nesting site, they encounter other dangers in the sea, from storms, pollution and from humans, who despite their endangered status, continue to rob their nests and kill them for meat. Most baby turtles don't live to reproduce.

The Kemp's Ridley is named after Richard M. Kemp, a fisherman, who first discovered them in Florida.

The Kemp's Ridley Sea Turtle is 61–91 cm long and weighs only 45 kg. This sea turtle has a rounded, greyish-greenish carapace. Its plastron (bottom shell) is yellowish in colour.

Kemp's Ridley Sea Turtles have an interesting nesting behaviour. Nesting occurs from May–July. Large numbers of Kemp's Ridleys gather off the nesting site and then arrive upon the beach in huge groups called arribadas, which is Spanish for 'arrival'. Scientists are not sure how these arribadas are triggered, but speculate offshore winds, lunar (moon) cycles or a release of pheromones by females as the cause.

These sea turtles primarily eat crabs, but also eat fish, jellyfish and molluscs.

MARINE REPTILES

Leatherback Sea Turtle

Leatherback Sea Turtles are the largest living turtles in the world. Adults usually range from 1.8-2.4 m in length and weigh 295 to 545 kg. This species has its throat lined with backward-pointing spines, an adaptation that enables it to feed extensively on jellyfish. Leatherbacks are primarily pelagic animals.

They travel great distances from their nesting beaches to their feeding grounds. Although Leatherbacks are most often found in tropical waters, they are distributed around the globe in temperate oceans, and even on the edges of subarctic water. The Leatherback Sea Turtle travels further north than any other sea turtle.

They live in Northern Atlantic waters as far north as Newfoundland, Nova Scotia and Labrador. They also inhabit South Atlantic waters, as far south as Argentina and South Africa. This turtle inhabits waters as far east as Britain and Norway. The biggest ever recorded Leatherback Turtle was a male stranded on a Welsh beach that reached 256 cm long and weighed 916 kg. A Leatherback was recorded to have descended to a maximum depth of 1,230 m, which represents the deepest dive ever recorded for a reptile.

Leatherbacks' diet consists mainly of jellyfish, and they have long, angled spines in their throats to keep their slippery prey from escaping. Since jellyfish eat fish larvae, leatherbacks play an important role in balancing the marine ecosystem by keeping jellyfish numbers under control and thereby preserve fish populations.

Olive Ridley Sea Turtle

The Olive Ridley is considered the most abundant sea turtle in the world, with an estimated 800,000 nesting females annually. The Olive Ridley gets its name from the greyish green colouration of its heart-shaped carapace (top shell).

Adult turtles are relatively small, weighing on average around 45 kg. The size and morphology of the Olive Ridley varies from region to region. The Olive Ridley has one of the most extraordinary nesting habits in the natural world. Large groups of turtles gather offshore of nesting beaches. Then, all at once, vast numbers of turtles come ashore and nest in what is known as an 'arribada'. During these arribadas, hundreds to thousands of females come ashore to lay their eggs. At many nesting beaches, the nesting density is so high that previously laid egg clutches are dug up by other females excavating the nest to lay their own eggs.

The Olive Ridley is omnivorous, meaning it feeds on a wide variety of food items, including algae, lobster, crabs, tunicates, molluscs, shrimp, and fish. Olive Ridleys are globally distributed in the tropical regions of the South Atlantic, Pacific and Indian Oceans. In the South Atlantic Ocean, they are found along the Atlantic coasts of West Africa and South America. In the Eastern Pacific, they occur from Southern California to Northern Chile.

MARINE REPTILES

Olive Sea Snake

The Olive Sea Snake is perhaps the commonest true sea snake in the tropical waters south of Papua New Guinea. It inhabits coral reefs and rocky coastlines to depths of upto 45 m.

Its upper body is purplish grey or dark brown, and the head is light to medium brown. Commonly, though not always, there are creamy scales along the body. The head is short and of equal width as the stocky body. The nostrils are valved, thus preventing water ingress. The tail is paddle-shaped with a raised ridge running along its length. The eyes are small.

As with all true sea snakes, live young are born at sea. Adults need to surface every half an hour to breathe fresh air. The species feeds on fish and crustaceans, and is active both day and night.

The Olive Sea Snake is highly venomous and should be treated with caution, though in reality they are generally not aggressive in temperament. Bites from the Olive Sea Snakes are rare.

The Olive Sea Snake occurs in the Timor Sea, throughout the Northern and North-eastern coasts of Australia, and in the Coral Sea and other areas south of Papua New Guinea.

Olive Ridley Sea Turtle

The Olive Ridley is considered the most abundant sea turtle in the world, with an estimated 800,000 nesting females annually. The Olive Ridley gets its name from the greyish green colouration of its heart-shaped carapace (top shell).

Adult turtles are relatively small, weighing on average around 45 kg. The size and morphology of the Olive Ridley varies from region to region. The Olive Ridley has one of the most extraordinary nesting habits in the natural world. Large groups of turtles gather offshore of nesting beaches. Then, all at once, vast numbers of turtles come ashore and nest in what is known as an 'arribada'. During these arribadas, hundreds to thousands of females come ashore to lay their eggs. At many nesting beaches, the nesting density is so high that previously laid egg clutches are dug up by other females excavating the nest to lay their own eggs.

The Olive Ridley is omnivorous, meaning it feeds on a wide variety of food items, including algae, lobster, crabs, tunicates, molluscs, shrimp, and fish. Olive Ridleys are globally distributed in the tropical regions of the South Atlantic, Pacific and Indian Oceans. In the South Atlantic Ocean, they are found along the Atlantic coasts of West Africa and South America. In the Eastern Pacific, they occur from Southern California to Northern Chile.

MARINE REPTILES

Olive Sea Snake

The Olive Sea Snake is perhaps the commonest true sea snake in the tropical waters south of Papua New Guinea. It inhabits coral reefs and rocky coastlines to depths of upto 45 m.

Its upper body is purplish grey or dark brown, and the head is light to medium brown. Commonly, though not always, there are creamy scales along the body. The head is short and of equal width as the stocky body. The nostrils are valved, thus preventing water ingress. The tail is paddle-shaped with a raised ridge running along its length. The eyes are small.

As with all true sea snakes, live young are born at sea. Adults need to surface every half an hour to breathe fresh air. The species feeds on fish and crustaceans, and is active both day and night.

The Olive Sea Snake is highly venomous and should be treated with caution, though in reality they are generally not aggressive in temperament. Bites from the Olive Sea Snakes are rare.

The Olive Sea Snake occurs in the Timor Sea, throughout the Northern and North-eastern coasts of Australia, and in the Coral Sea and other areas south of Papua New Guinea.

Some well-known marine reptiles

Beaked Sea Snake

Notoriously aggressive and readily provoked, this widespread species is responsible for nine out of every ten deaths from sea-snake bites. Light gray with indistinct blue-gray bands, it has a sharply pointed head, slender body and paddle like tail. Its fangs are less than 4 mm long, but its jaws can gape widely to accommodate large prey. It feeds mainly on catfish and shrimp. Swimming near the bottom in shallow, murky water, in coastal waters, mangrove swamps, estuaries and rivers, it locates its victims by smell and touch. Like all fish-eating snakes, it waits until its prey has stopped struggling, before turning it so that it can be consumed head-first.

Beaked Sea Snakes give birth to up to 30 young each time they breed, but their mortality is high, and only a small proportion of the young survive to become parents themselves. Despite their venom, these snakes are eaten by inshore predators, such as fish and estuarine crocodiles.

The Beaked Sea Snake's bite contains enough venom to kill 50 people—about twice as many as the most venomous terrestrial snakes, such as the King Cobra or Death Adder. Most of the snake's human victims are bitten when wading or fishing in muddy water. However, its deadly venom does not protect this snake from being caught in shrimp-trawling nets. This hazard affects many sea snakes, but the Beaked Sea Snake is particularly susceptible because it lives in shallow water and eats shrimp.

Banded Sea Snake

Banded Sea Snake is normally docile to humans but its venom is highly dangerous. They are blue or blue gray in colour with approximately 20-65 black bands. They can grow up to 2 m in length. The underneath flesh of the snake is yellow or cream in colour. The snout and upper lips are usually yellow in colour. The compressed tail helps it to move speedily in the water. Banded Sea Snake is also known by other names including large scaled sea krait or banded sea krait.

There are over fifty species of Banded Sea Snakes. Some of the sea snakes produce venomous poison that can be lethal to humans. Majority of the sea snakes are not aggressive unless you severely mistreat them. On an average the sea snake can produce 10-15 mg of venom with one bite strike. If it injects 15 mg of venom, the victim may die immediately due to the speed of the poison spreading in the blood system. Black banded sea snake kraits are known to be extremely poisonous. They often remain in the reefs for a long time to hunt for prey. When they spot a prey, they would bite the prey and inject the poison so that it becomes paralyzed.

Poisonous Banded Sea Snakes are usually found on the island of Fiji. They are widely distributed in the tropical Indo Pacific Ocean. They like to lurk around the coastal waters of the islands and barrier reefs.

Some well-known marine reptiles

Yellow-bellied Sea Snake

The Yellow-bellied sea snake has a prominent paddle-like tail. The snake's colouration normally includes a black background colour contrasting strongly with a yellow belly and pale yellow lateral stripe along the body which frequently breaks into an undulating array of black and yellow blotches on the posterior body and tail.

This snake spends much of its time floating in open ocean waters along the edges of the continental shelves of large land masses. It is a member of the largest sea snake family, Hydrophiidae, and hence bears its young alive without leaving the ocean.

This boldly striped yellow-and-black snake has venom that is more toxic than that of a cobra. It is also the world's most wide-ranging snake and one of the very few that lives in the surface waters of the open ocean. Its distinctive colours warn that it is poisonous, protecting it from many predators. It feeds on small fish trying to shelter in its shade, swimming forward or backward with equal ease to grab them with its jaws. Although its fangs are tiny, its potent venom occasionally causes human fatalities.

At sea, these snakes may form vast flotillas, hundreds of thousands strong, and after storms, they may be washed up on beaches that lie far outside their normal range. However, the species has never managed to colonize the Atlantic Ocean, because cold currents stand in its way. Yellow-bellied Sea Snakes give birth to up to six young each time they breed.

MARINE REPTILES

Some extinct marine reptiles

Mosasaur

Mosasaurs were serpentine marine lizards and ferocious predators. Mosasaurs were not dinosaurs but evolved from semi-aquatic squamates known as the 'aigialosaurs', close relatives of modern-day monitor lizards. Mosasaurs breathed air and were powerful swimmers that were well-adapted to living in the warm, shallow epicontinental seas prevalent during the Late Cretaceous Period. They grew up to 17 m long but the longest ever recorded Mosasaur was 17.5 m long.

Mosasaurs were serpentine marine reptiles. The first fossil remains were discovered in a limestone quarry at Maastricht on the Meuse in 1764. These ferocious marine predators are now considered to be the closest relatives of snakes.

Mosasaurs ate large fish, shellfish, sharks and some even ate mollusks. They lived during the same period Tyrannosaurus rex roamed the earth. Mosasaurs can easily be considered the Tyrannosaurus rex of the prehistoric seas! Such creatures were true hunter-killers that had no rival during their existence.

Mosasaur remains have been found in many regions all over the globe.

Some extinct marine reptiles

Elasmosaurus

Elasmosaurus was a long-necked marine reptile that was up to 14 m long. Half of its length was its neck, which had as many as 75-76 vertebrae in it (in comparison, people have 7-8 neck vertebrae). Elasmosaurus had four long, paddle-like flippers, a tiny head, sharp teeth in strong jaws and a pointed tail. It was the longest of the Plesiosaurs.

Elasmosaurus lived during the Late Cretaceous Period, and went extinct during the K-T mass extinction (65 million years ago). Elasmosaurus lived in the open oceans and breathed air. Some Elasmosaurus have been found with small stones in their stomachs; these may have been used to help grind up their food, or as ballast, to help them dive.

Elasmosaurus ate fish and other swimming animals. They had strong jaws and sharp teeth. Elasmosaurus swam slowly using its four paddle-like flippers in a manner similar to that of modern turtles. It may have been able to move a little bit on sandy shores, perhaps to lay its eggs.

Elasmosaurus was named by palaeontologist E. D. Cope in 1868 (from a fossil found in Wyoming, USA). Other Elasmosaurus fossils have also been found in North America.

MARINE REPTILES

Keichousaurus

Keichousaurus was an early reptile that lived during the Triassic Period (roughly 245-208 Ma). The animal was small, about 15-30 cm (6-12 in) long, with a long neck and tail, five-toed feet with long digits, and a pointed head with sharp teeth.

Fossils have been found in Guizhou Province, China, and are popular with collectors, principally because complete articulated skeletons are relatively common from this area, and frequently advertised for sale.

The usual species encountered for sale is Keichousaurus hui.

The most prominent example of the obscure reptile order known as pachypleurosauria, Keichousaurus is among the oldest of all marine reptiles, and may have been ancestral to the huge plesiosaurs and pliosaurs of the Jurassic and Cretaceous Periods. Palaeontologists believe Keichousaurus spent most of its time in the water, but may have been able to crawl occasionally onto land with its strong front legs.

Because it was so small, Keichousaurus fossilized unusually well—it's not uncommon to find complete, articulated skeletons of this reptile embedded in rock, which are prized (and expensive) collector's items.

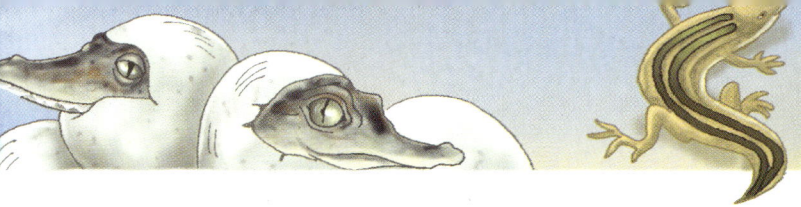

Some extinct marine reptiles

Nothosaurs

Nothosaurs were long-necked, long-tailed, fish-eating reptiles ranging from a few inches to 6 m long. Nothosaurs had four wide, paddle-like limbs with webbed fingers and toes. These reptiles had a long, thin head with many sharp teeth; the front teeth were longer than the back teeth. The nostrils were on the top end of the snout. They breathed air but spent most of the time in the water.

Nothosaurs fossils were found all over the world. They breathed air but it's obvious that they spent most of their time in water, except to lay eggs. The Nothosaurs are also known to be the earliest sea-living reptilian hunters of the waters. Nothosaurs lived during the Triassic Period, and went extinct during the Late Triassic Period. They may have evolved into the plesiosaurs.

Nothosaurs ate fish and other small swimming animals like shrimp. They fished using their sharp teeth and long snout. Some of the best preserved fossils preserved their skin and the drawing shows that Nothosaurus had webbed feet, suitable for both the aquatic environment and land.

MARINE REPTILES

Archelon

The Giant Turtle Archelon was a slow moving creature of the ancient seas during the Cretaceous Period (65 to 146 million years ago). Some remains measure over 4.9 m long. Like many of today's turtles it ate jellyfish and drifting fish as well as plants, buried its eggs in sandy beaches, and may have lived for more than 100 years.

The first remains of Archelon were discovered by D. Wieland in the year 1895 near South Dakota. It is assumed that the closest relative of this giant turtle is the Leatherback Turtle.

The physical features of the Archelon invoke awe and wonder. Though it was gigantic it did not possess a very hard shell. Instead, it had a framework that was absolutely skeletal. It had a tail that aided it in swimming along with the flippers. The Archelon's bite was so hard that it could smash any hard thing to dust within a second. It was assumed that the favourite marine species after its choice was the squid.

Its name means 'ancient turtle' and when it was discovered, it was the oldest and most primitive large sea turtle fossil yet discovered. In recent decades, other specimens of this and other ancient turtle species have come to light that show Archelon as part of an already well developed order of animals.

In fact, this creature evolved around 150 million years after the first primitive turtle ancestors.

Some extinct marine reptiles

Nothosaurs

Nothosaurs were long-necked, long-tailed, fish-eating reptiles ranging from a few inches to 6 m long. Nothosaurs had four wide, paddle-like limbs with webbed fingers and toes. These reptiles had a long, thin head with many sharp teeth; the front teeth were longer than the back teeth. The nostrils were on the top end of the snout. They breathed air but spent most of the time in the water.

Nothosaurs fossils were found all over the world. They breathed air but it's obvious that they spent most of their time in water, except to lay eggs. The Nothosaurs are also known to be the earliest sea-living reptilian hunters of the waters. Nothosaurs lived during the Triassic Period, and went extinct during the Late Triassic Period. They may have evolved into the plesiosaurs.

Nothosaurs ate fish and other small swimming animals like shrimp. They fished using their sharp teeth and long snout. Some of the best preserved fossils preserved their skin and the drawing shows that Nothosaurus had webbed feet, suitable for both the aquatic environment and land.

MARINE REPTILES

Archelon

The Giant Turtle Archelon was a slow moving creature of the ancient seas during the Cretaceous Period (65 to 146 million years ago). Some remains measure over 4.9 m long. Like many of today's turtles it ate jellyfish and drifting fish as well as plants, buried its eggs in sandy beaches, and may have lived for more than 100 years.

The first remains of Archelon were discovered by D. Wieland in the year 1895 near South Dakota. It is assumed that the closest relative of this giant turtle is the Leatherback Turtle.

The physical features of the Archelon invoke awe and wonder. Though it was gigantic it did not possess a very hard shell. Instead, it had a framework that was absolutely skeletal. It had a tail that aided it in swimming along with the flippers. The Archelon's bite was so hard that it could smash any hard thing to dust within a second. It was assumed that the favourite marine species after its choice was the squid.

Its name means 'ancient turtle' and when it was discovered, it was the oldest and most primitive large sea turtle fossil yet discovered. In recent decades, other specimens of this and other ancient turtle species have come to light that show Archelon as part of an already well developed order of animals.

In fact, this creature evolved around 150 million years after the first primitive turtle ancestors.

Test Your MEMORY

1. What are reptiles?

2. Write briefly about the evolution of reptiles.

3. What are marine reptiles?

4. Write about the classification of marine reptiles.

5. Write about the habitats of marine reptiles.

6. Describe the food habits of marine reptiles.

7. Write some of the characteristics of marine reptiles.

8. Write briefly about the Saltwater Crocodile.

9. Write briefly about the Marine Iguana.

10. Write a few lines about the Leatherback Sea Turtle.

11. Describe briefly the Banded Sea Snake.

12. Describe briefly the Mosasaur.

Index

A

algae 9, 11, 13, 21
Amniota 5
amniotic eggs 15
Anapsids 6
Archelon 30
Archosaurs 6

B

Banded Sea Snake 24
Beaked Sea Snake 23

C

cloaca 16

D

Diapsids 6

E

ectothermic 3
Elasmosaurus 27

F

Flatback Sea Turtle 18

G

Galapagos Marine Iguana 8, 9, 11, 13

H

Hylonomus 5

K

Keichousaurus 28
Kemp's Ridley Sea Turtle 19
keratin 14

L

Leatherback Sea Turtle 20
Lepidosaurs 6

M

metabolism 17
Mosasaurs 7, 26

N

Nothosaurs 29

O

Olive Ridley Sea Turtle 21
Olive Sea Snake 22

S

Saltwater crocodile 3, 7, 8, 9, 12, 13, 18
scutes 14
sea snakes 7, 8, 12, 22, 23, 24, 25
sea turtle 6, 7, 8, 9, 10, 11, 12, 13, 16, 18, 19, 20, 21, 30
Synapsids 6

T

tetrapods 4, 15, 17

V

vertebrates 3, 4, 5

Y

Yellow-bellied Sea Snake 13, 25